A MIGHTY WIND

THE ILLUSTRATED SONGBOOK

Introduction by
CHRISTOPHER GUEST

A Perigee Book

CASTLE ROCK ENTERTAINMENT PRESENTS "A MIGHTY WIND" BOB BALABAN CHRISTOPHER GUEST JOHN MICHAEL HIGGINS EUGENE LEVY JANE LYNCH MICHAEL McKEAN CATHERINE O'HAR PARKER POSEY HARRY SHEARER FRED WILLARD MUSIC PRODUCED BY C.J. VANSTON EDITED BY ROBERT LEIGHTON PRODUCTION DESIGNER JOSEPH T. GARRITY DIRECTOR OF PHOTOGRAPHY ARLENE DONNELLY NELSON

CASTLE ROCK 7 Sex-Related Humor PRODUCED BY KAREN MURPHY WRITTEN BY CHRISTOPHER GUEST & EUGENE LEVY DIRECTED BY CHRISTOPHER GUEST CC WARNER BROS. PICTURES A WARNER BROS. ENTERTAINMENT COMPANY

www.amightywindonline.com   America Online Keyword: A Mighty Wind   www.castle-rock.com   www.warnervideo.com

ORIGINAL SONGS WRITTEN / PERFORMED BY: CHRISTOPHER GUEST / JOHN MICHAEL HIGGINS / EUGENE LEVY / MICHAEL McKEAN / CATHERINE O'HARA / ANNETTE O'TOOLE / HARRY SHEARER / C.J. VANSTON
SOUNDTRACK ALBUM ON DMZ/COLUMBIA/SONY MUSIC SOUNDTRAX

ACKNOWLEDGMENTS

This Illustrated Songbook came about because of so many talented people.

The wonderful, catchy folk songs were written by Christopher Guest, Eugene Levy, Harry Shearer, Michael McKean, Annette O'Toole, Catherine O'Hara, CJ Vanston, and John Michael Higgins.

Inspired by the music and humming along, Karen Murphy edited and compiled the songbook.

Tom Halm, CJ Vanston, and Dave Blasucci perfectly added their musical expertise.

Dave Park, Joe Garrity, and Digital Fusion created the album cover artistry.

Suzanne Tenner, Joe Pugliese, and Art Streiber, great photographers, took the pictures.

Jess Wittenberg, Margo Meyer, Pam Griner, Stephanie Sea, Mick Meyhew, Steve Younger, Sam Fusco, and Katy Fox helped with hard work and great ideas.

Martin Shafer and the folks at Castle Rock Entertainment gave their enthusiatic support.

Bill Bentley and David Zimmer made the Penguin connection.

Julie Merberg and her team beautifully produced the book, and John Duff, publisher and editor extraordinaire was the tasteful guide.

A Perigee Book
Published by The Berkley Publishing Group
A division of Penguin Group (USA) Inc.
375 Hudson Street
New York, New York 10014

© 2003 Castle Rock Entertainment.
Text design by pink design, inc.
Cover design by pink design, inc.
(www.pinkdesigninc.com)

ISBN: 0-399-52983-7

Visit the Penguin Group (USA) web site at:
www.penguin.com

A Roundtable Press Book

First edition: November 2003

This title has been cataloged by the Library of Congress

Printed in the United States of America
10 9 8 7 6 5 4 3 2 1

CONTENTS

Mitch & Mickey

Introduction

The creaking sound at the wharf came from the boats as they rubbed against the dock. In the distance a foghorn moaned in a lonely way. The detective was still out cold. The fist that had knocked him out was now in the pocket of a man speeding away in a black coupe.

— *Ira Beyman,* The Tree of Dr.Kell

It is almost a certainty that tens of thousands of years ago, men and women living in caves, hollowed-out tree trunks, and other unacceptable dwellings told stories to each other. What they didn't know then, and don't know now because they are dead, is that they were, minus the turtlenecks, guitars, and capos, the first troubadours. It is a proud tradition that has continued through the ages. When music entered the equation is difficult to say with absolute certainty, but it was probably around the 1920s. Or much earlier, say, the 1600s.

Thankfully, through the oral traditions of many cultures and the Brill Building, many of these stories survive in fully protected copyright form. They are our connection to the past. Perhaps that is why folk music has never been very far from our hearts and minds. It is truly everyman's music, and everyman can be heard singing it the world over. Although it helps to be poor, in terms of credibility, no one race or religion has a patent on this kind of music. It is the world's heritage.

The songs in this collection are the work of many different writers, musicians, and actors. While the styles may vary from traditional to pretentious to just plain strange, they do have one thing in common. They are part of a legacy. Just what kind of legacy is up to you, the public, and the many agents and managers who represent these individuals.

I predict that a thousand years from now, young and old will still be singing these same songs, whether asked to or not.

— *Christopher Guest*

The Folksmen

The New Main Street Singers

The FOLKSMEN

Mark was the baritone, born in Kadota, Minnesota, named for pioneering Midwestern farmers who had ventured west and returned home with an ill-fated plan to grow the fig seedlings they brought back with them. Alan was the tenor, from upstate New York farm country, a quiet man with an even quieter way about him. Jerry was the missing link.

In 1961 the Twobadors, Alan Barrows and Mark Shubb, forsook their comfy fame as the University of Vermont's best-known folk duo to take the fateful bus trip to New York City. There, in Greenwich Village's dilapidated but already legendary Folk Place, the leading lights of the burgeoning pop-folk movement, and those who aspired to join them, "hooted" onstage from evening deep into the early morn.

On their first, nervous visit to the Folk Place, Mark and Alan spotted a young, handsome fellow playing guitar and singing in a strong midrange voice. His name, he said just before he left the stage to make way for headliners Mitch & Mickey, was Jerry Palter.

Alan and Mark had found their lead singer, and the Folksmen were born. Pioneering folk manager Irving Steinbloom, known in the business as the Man with the Golden Ear, signed the fledgling trio to Folktown Records, and the 'Men were on their way, enjoying a ride that was as dizzying on the way up as on the way down.

In the decade to follow, the trio toured continuously, made numerous television appearances, hit the pop charts (number 17) with their infectious, good-time sing-along "Old Joe's Place," and became perennial residents in the nation's folk bins with such albums as *Ramblin', Singin', Pickin', Hitchin',* and *Wishin'*. In 1968 they became one of the last folk bands to experiment with amplified music, breaking their one-word-title rule with the pensive electric collection *Saying Something*. It was from that album that the Folksmen's last chart entry, "Childen of the Sun," rose to bubbling-under status on Billboard's short-lived folk-rock chart.

1965

1965

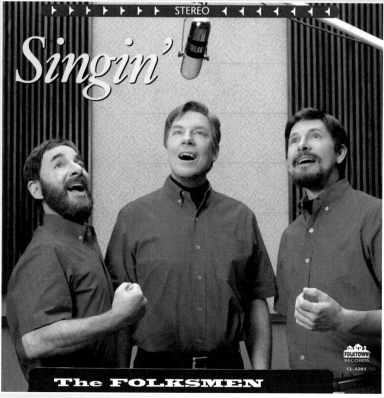

1966

1967

1967

1968 The trio's one and only experiment using electric instruments.

The
FOLKSMEN
Reunion BBQ
Pine Falls, New York
2003

Mitch & Mickey

The phenomenon of that kiss
can't be overstated.
It was a superb moment in
the history of folk music,
and maybe a great moment
in the history of humans.

— *Martin Berg, folk historian*

Every poet has a muse, and Mitch Cohen was no different. It took the destined meeting with fellow folk musician Mickey Devlin for Mitch to realize his full potential as a poet/songwriter. From then on they became known as Mitch & Mickey, the darlings and icons of the 1960s folk music scene. Together they were a singular energy beyond comparison, releasing such beloved albums as *Meet Mitch & Mickey, When You're Next to Me, Over the Moon,* and *Together Forever,* to name a few. It was a shock to everyone when it was announced that Mitch and Mickey had ended their collaborative and romantic relationship. Their breakup catapulted Mitch into a prolonged depression. And now that Mitch and Mickey have reunited, audiences are again eagerly awaiting their performances.

meet
Mitch & Mickey

CR-26015

1965
Their first album,
it contained the hit
single "Kiss at the
End of the Rainbow."

◄ ◄ ◄ ◄ ◄ STEREOPHONIC SOUND ► ► ► ► ►

Songs From A Love Nest

Mitch & Mickey

CR-25465

1966

STEREO

If This Rose
Could Talk

Mitch
&
Mickey

PR-3798

1966

1967

1967

The first group to have a "Greatest Hits" songbook after only two years.

1968

1968

STEREO

Mitch & Mickey

CR-00016

STEREO

Over the Moon

Mitch & Mickey

1969

Their least successful album.

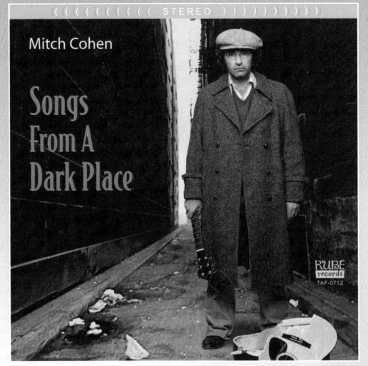

1971

The first of Mitch's solo (post-Mickey) albums.

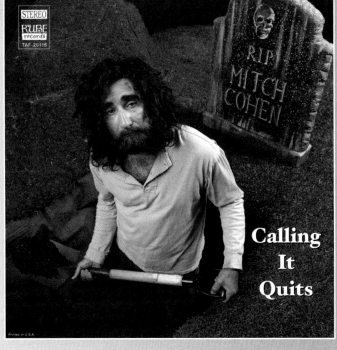

1972

Known as the album with no content.

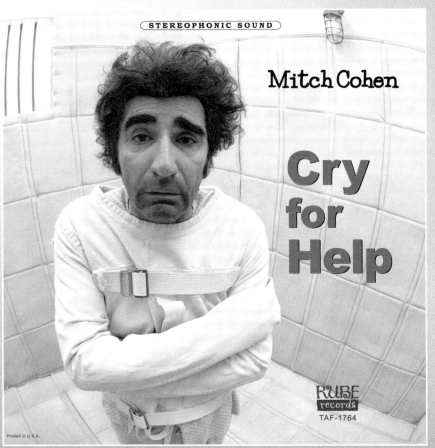

1973

Mitch's last album before extended stint at sanitarium.

20

I think we were easy to love, in a way, because we represented true love and romance and sweetness, and, to be quite honest, I bought the image as much as anyone else....'Cause it was sweet and happy, and everybody loved to hang around Mitch, you know....

— *Mickey, on Mitch & Mickey's popularity*

Rock Port Folk Festival

Lee Aikman's Folk Hour, 1966

Mitch & Mickey's guest appearance on "Dick Beyman Private Eye" TV show in the late 60s

*Together again
2003*

THE NEW MAIN STREET SINGERS

One night in 1960, I'll never forget this, we were at a hootenanny and we were jamming with the Klapper family. And all of a sudden, I heard it: this sound that I had been thinking about.

The harmonics were amazing. I thought, well there's five of us and four of them—it's a neuftet.... Well, this thing clicked with the Klappers, too. So we joined forces, and we became the Main Street Singers.

— George Menschell, describing the fateful evening that his band, the Village Folk Ensemble, merged with the Klappers to become the Main Street Singers

The Main Street Singers, 1961

A year after this seminal moment in folk history, the Main Street Singers released their first album, *Strolling Down Main Street*. The group would become a virtual record-making machine, producing 30 albums in just under a decade before breaking up in 1971. It would take a chance meeting between Menschell and Mike LaFontaine of Hi-Class Management at Fort Lauderdale's Laff Pit Comedy Club in 1980 to bring the band back together. LaFontaine, a borderline celebrity in his own right, saw gold for a brand name as recognizable as the Main Street Singers. Today they are the New Main Street Singers, and Menschell has handed the band's day-to-day activities to Terry and Laurie Bohner—a spirited couple who can carry any slot in the neuftet range, coordinate the band's uniforms, manage their schedule, and still have time to chair the Tampa chapter of W.I.N.C. (Witches in Nature's Colors).

The New Main Street Singers, 2003

THE BAND'S GENEALOGY

1957

BALLADEERS	VILLAGERS	Ramblin'
George Menschell	Fred Knox	Sandy
Chuck Wiseman	Bill Weyburn	Pitnik

1958
THE VILLAGE FOLK ENSEMBLE
George Menschell   Chuck Wiseman
Fred Knox   Bill Weyburn
Ramblin' Sandy Pitnik

1960
THE KLAPPERS
Ma Pa Boy Girl

1961
THE MAIN STREET SINGERS
George Menschell   Chuck Wiseman
Fred Knox   Bill Weyburn
Ramblin' Sandy Pitnik
The Klapper Family

1971
The Main Street Singers break up

1980
The New Main Street Singers are formed

1980	1983	1989	1995	2003
George Menschell	George Menschell	George Menschell	George Menschell	George Menschell
Fred Knox	Fred Knox	Fred Knox	Terry Bohner	Terry Bohner
Larry Rogow	Terry Bohner	Terry Bohner	Laurie Bohner	Laurie Bohner
Ed Forde	Laurie Bohner	Laurie Bohner	Sissy Knox	Sissy Knox
Bud Murphy	Kyle Ham	Chris Holt	Jerald Smithers	Tony Pollono
Adam Sayers	Bill Yoelin	Roger Webster	Andrew Dickler	Jerald Smithers
Sara Newberry	Sara Newberry	Natalie Lehmann	Mike Maryama	Mike Maryama
Shelly Owen	Seth Segal	Mark Yoshikawa	Sam Blasucci	Johnny Athenakis
Matt Murray	George Bours	Robby Fisher	Johnny Athenakis	Sean Halloran

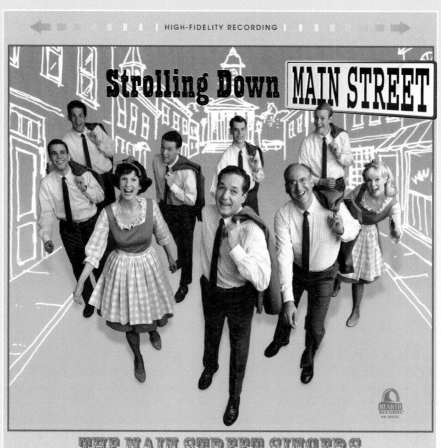

1961

1964

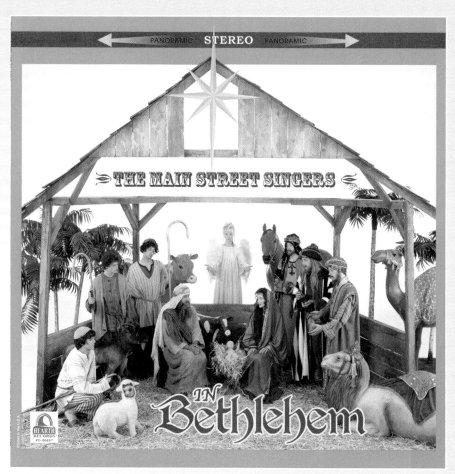

1966

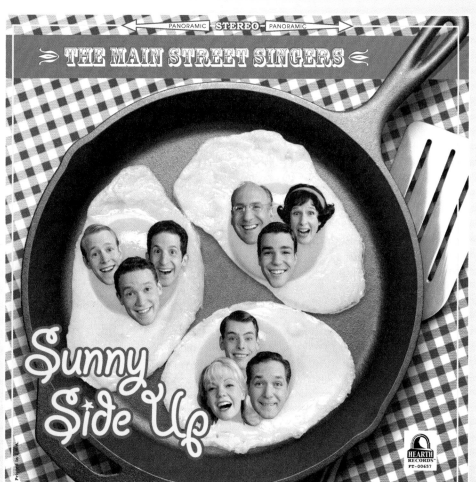

1967

I tell you, my head opened up, my heart opened up. I listened to that record over and over and over. I knew it right, left, and every way to Sunday. I felt like I knew those people.

— Terry Bohner, on his discovery, as a child,
of the Main Street Singers' song "Sunny Side Up"

And I loved to sing, ever since I was a little girl. And I learned to play ukelele in one of my last films, Not So Tiny Tim, *and based on that, my world opened up, because I was invited to join the re-formed New Main Street Singers.*

— Laurie Bohner

A MIGHTY WIND
THE SONGS

Barnyard Symphony

Words and Music by
CHRISTOPHER GUEST

Blood on the Coal

Words and Music by
CHRISTOPHER GUEST
MICHAEL McKEAN and
HARRY SHEARER

Blood on the Coal *continued*

Blood on the Coal *continued*

Now an Ir - ish - man____ named Mur - phy said____ "I'll

stop that i - ron horse"____ As he stood ath - wart____its pas - sage____ and it

crushed him dead, of course____ And I hope he hears the i - ro - ny____ when e'er____

____ this tale is told That the train that took his life____ was burn - ing

good Ken - tuck - y coal *(Hey!)* Blood on the tracks Blood in the mine

Broth - ers and sis - ters, what a ter - ri - ble time Old nine - ty - sev - en got

in the wrong____ hole Now in mine num - ber six - ty there's blood on the coal____

(Blood on the coal____ Blood on the coal)____

Children of the Sun

Words and Music by
CHRISTOPHER GUEST
MICHAEL McKEAN and
HARRY SHEARER

Children of the Sun *continued*

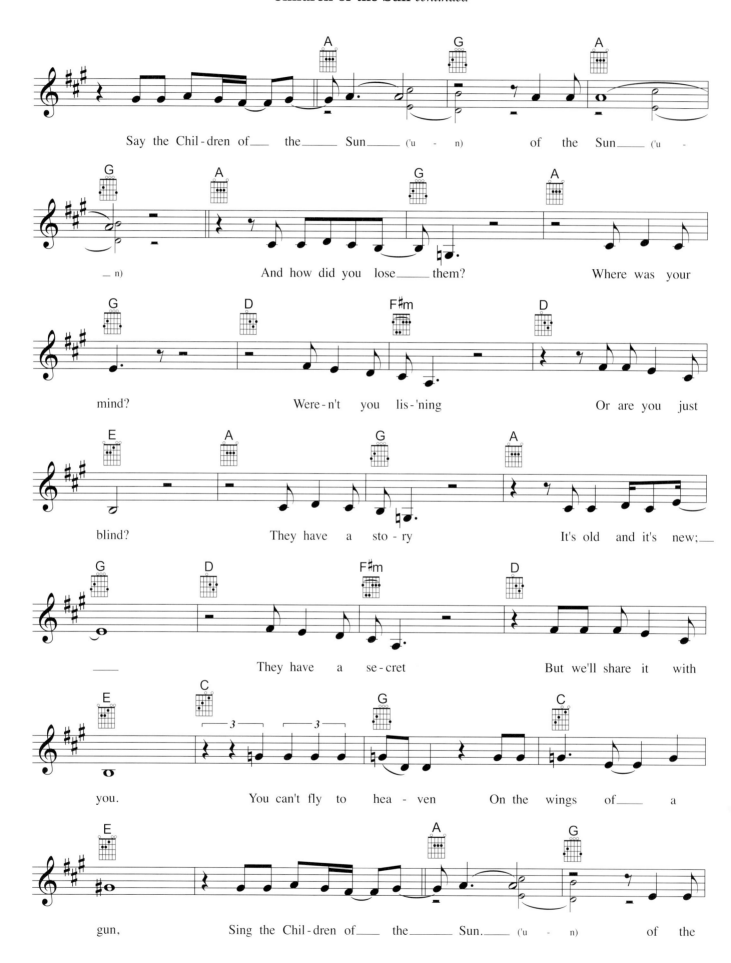

Children of the Sun *continued*

(Instrumental)

Sun._____ ('u – – n)

Our num - ber is

man - y, Our voice is____ as one, Quoth the Chil-dren of____ the____

____ Sun.____ ('u – n) of the____ Sun.____ ('u – n) The Chil-dren of____ the____

____ Sun.____ ('u – n) of the Sun.____ ('u – n) The Chil-dren of____ the____

Repeat and Fade

____ Sun.

Corn Wine

Words and Music by
HARRY SHEARER

Corn Wine *continued*

hus-band starts a-work-in' At the ros-y crack of dawn And hey non-ny no, non-ny nin-ny oh

He comes home and mows the lawn___ A moth-er gives her child-ren The

things she nev-er had It's hey non-ny no, non-ny nin-ny oh Then

all they miss is Dad Con-sid-er the corn,___ con-sid-er the wine___

One has a day when it's in its prime The oth-er takes years to be sturd-y and fine If

on-ly the two could in-ter - twine. Corn wine, corn___ wine An

old man sits think-in' 'Bout the game his life has played. It's hey non-ny no, non-ny nin-ny oh

Corn Wine *continued*

He needs both nurse and maid An old wo-man's_ tak-in' care of

One she's loved so long It's hey non-ny no, non-ny nin-ny oh_____ And an

end-ing for this song Con - sid-er the corn,___ con-sid-er the wine___

One's in a hur-ry, the oth-er takes time One's on a stalk, the oth-er's on a vine If

on-ly the two could just com - bine Corn wine, corn___

wine *rit.* corn_____ wine.

Loco Man

Words and Music by
HARRY SHEARER

Never Did No Wanderin'

Words and Music by
MICHAEL McKEAN and
HARRY SHEARER

Never Did No Wanderin' *continued*

all

They say the high-way's just one big road___ And it goes from here to there___ And they

say you car - ry a hea-vy load When you're roll-in' down the line some - where___

___ Nev - er seen the dance___ of the tel - e - phone___ poles As they go whiz-zin'

by___ No I nev-er did no wan - derin'___ Nev - er did no

wan - derin'___ Nev-er did no wan-derin' af - ter all

Nev - er did no wan - der-in' high___

Nev - er did no wan - der-in' low___

Never Did No Wanderin' *continued*

Now a sail-or's life___ is a life for him But it nev-er was___ for me___ And I've

nev-er soared___where the hawk may soar___ Or seen what the hawk may see___

___ Nev-er hiked to heav - en on a moun-tain trail Nev-er rode on a riv-er's

rage___ No I nev-er did no wan - derin'___

Nev-er did no wan - derin'___ Nev-er did no wan-derin' af - ter

all Nev-er did no wan-derin' af - ter all

Old Joe's Place

Words and Music by
CHRISTOPHER GUEST
MICHAEL McKEAN and
HARRY SHEARER

When- ev - er I'm___ out wan - der - in'___
Chas- in' a rain - bow dream I of - ten stop and think a - bout___ a
place I've nev - er seen Where friend - ly folks can gath - er___ and
raise the raf - ters high With songs and tales of yes - ter - year___ Until they say good - bye Well___ there's a

Old Joe's Place *continued*

pup - py in the par - lor and a skil - let on the stove and a smel - ly old blan - ket that a

Nav - a - jo wove There's chick - en on the ta - ble but you got - ta say grace There's

al - ways some - thing cook - in' at Old Joe's Place

Now folks come 'round 'bout

eve - nin' time Soon as the sun goes down

Some drop in from right next door and some from out of town *"Pick it!"*

(Banjo solo)

Old Joe's Place *continued*

Well there's a pup - py in the par - lor and a

skil - let on the stove and a smel - ly old blan - ket that a Nav - a - jo wove There's

pop - corn in the pop - per and a pork - er in the pot There's pie in the pan - try and the

cof - fee's al - ways hot There's chic - ken on the ta - ble but you got - ta say grace There's

al - ways some - thing cook - in' at Old Joe's Place

Now they don't al - low no frowns in - side

Old Joe's Place *continued*

C			F		C	C/B	Am	Am/G

Leave them by the door___ There's ap-ple bran-dy by the keg___ and

D		G		Am		Em	

saw-dust on the floor___ So if you've got a hank-'rin'___ I'll

Am		G	G7	C		C/B	Am	Am/G

tell you where to go Just look for the bust-ed ne-on sign that

F		N.C.			

flash - es *Ea'* *a'* *'oe's*

accel. poco a poco

		F		C	

Well___ there's a pup-py in the par-lor and a

F	C	F	C	G	C

skil - let on the stove and a smel-ly old blan-ket that a Nav-a-jo wove There's

F	C	F	C	F	C

pop-corn in the pop-per and a pork-er in the pot There's pie in the pan-try and the

Old Joe's Place *continued*

cof-fee's al-ways hot There's sau-sage in the morn-ing and a par-ty ev-'ry night There's a

nurse on du-ty if you don't feel right There's chic-ken on the tab-le but you

Brisk tempo

got-ta say grace There's al-ways some-thing cook-in' at

Old Joe's Place

Skeletons of Quinto

Words and Music by
CHRISTOPHER GUEST

I worked the fields my fa-ther worked___ From dawn 'til set-ting sun

My cal-loused hands and wind-burned face___ Have marked me as a man___

Who has no voice, no___ rights, no hope No place to call his own And the

skel-e-tons___ of Quin-to call me home

(Spoken:) The sil-ver ten-ta-cles of the moon's rays haunt me

The death-ly si-lence of the moun-tains Chills me___ to the bone___ And the

Skeletons of Quinto *continued*

skel-e-tons___ of Quin-to call me home

If I live to be a hun-dred I won't know mi pa-pa's plight

The cruel-ty of the mast-er's whip___ The hor-rors of the night

He braved them all and stood his ground___ The brav-est ev-er known___ And the

skel-e-tons___ of Quin-to___ call me home

ad lib. Spanish recitative (additional verses on page 57)

(Nylon String Guitar solo—sounds 1 octave lower)

Skeletons of Quinto *continued*

I know that some-how in this world___ The work-ers must be free

That toil and sweat and ty-ran-ny,___ the fas-cist jeu d'es-prit

Will on-ly serve to keep us down___ and aid the bour-geoi-sie And the

skel-e-tons___ of Quin-to call me home

The FOLKSMEN SONG LYRICS

BARNYARD SYMPHONY
C. Guest

Every morn' at five o'clock
The farmer jumps out of bed
Washes up, ties his shoes,
Puts a hat upon his head

And the chickens cluck
The horses neigh
The crickets go fiddle-dee-dee
The bullfrog croaks
The pigs oink oink
It's a barnyard symphony

The sun goes down, his work is done
The farmer gets into bed
And in his dreams he hears the sounds
Of the barnyard in his head

And the chickens cluck
The horses neigh
The crickets go fiddle-dee-dee
The bullfrog croaks
The pigs oink oink
It's a barnyard symphony

BLOOD ON THE COAL
C. Guest, M. McKean & H. Shearer

It was April twenty-seventh
In the year of ninety-one
'Bout a mile below the surface
And the warm Kentucky sun

The late shift was ending
And the early shift was late
And the foreman ate his dinner
From a dirty tin plate

Blood on the tracks
Blood in the mine
Brothers and sisters, what a terrible time
Old '97 went in the wrong hole
Now in mine number sixty there's blood on the coal
Blood on the coal
Blood on the coal

Well the slag pits were steaming
It was 7:25
Every miner worked the coalface
Every one of them alive

The train came 'round the corner
You could hear the trestle groan
But the switcher wasn't listening
So he left the switch alone

Blood on the tracks
Blood in the mine
Brothers and sisters, what a terrible time
Old '97 went in the wrong hole
Now in mine number sixty there's blood on the coal
Blood on the coal
Blood on the coal

Well, the walls began to tremble
And the men began to yell
They could hear that lonesome whistle
Like an echo out of…well…

They dropped their picks and shovels
As to safety they did run
For to stay among the living
In the year of ninety-one

Blood on the tracks
Blood in the mine
Brothers and sisters, what a terrible time
Old '97 went in the wrong hole
Now in mine number sixty there's blood on the coal
Blood on the coal
Blood on the coal

Now an Irishman named Murphy
Said, "I'll stop that iron horse"
As he stood athwart its passage
And it crushed him dead, of course

And I hope he hears the irony
When e'er this tale is told
That the train that took his life was burning
Good Kentucky coal (Hey!)

Blood on the tracks
Blood in the mine
Brothers and sisters, what a terrible time
Old '97 got in the wrong hole
Now in mine number sixty there's blood on the coal
Blood on the coal
Blood on the coal

CHILDREN OF THE SUN
M. McKean, H. Shearer & C. Guest

Who are these young ones
So wild and so free?
Are they your sons and daughters
Could they ever be?

They show you a moonbeam
You call it a star;
They say come and join us
You stay where you are

The past is behind you
The future's begun,
Say the Children of the Sun

And how did you lose them?
Where was your mind?
Weren't you listening
Or are you just blind?

They have a story
It's old and it's new
They have a secret
But we'll share it with you.

You can't fly to heaven
On the wings of a gun,
Sing the Children of the Sun

Our number is many,
Our voice is as one,
Quoth the Children of the Sun

CORN WINE
H. Shearer

A young man goes courtin'
With just one thing in mind
It's hey nonny no, nonny ninny oh
A good time for to find

A young girl starts a-flirtin'
With just one tale to tell
It's hey nonny no, nonny ninny oh
A man to wed her well

Consider the corn, consider the wine
One's in a hurry, the other takes time
One's on a stalk, the other's on a vine
If only the two could just combine
Corn wine, corn wine

A husband starts a-workin'
At the rosy crack of dawn
And hey nonny no, nonny ninny oh
He comes home and mows the lawn

A mother gives her children
The things she never had
It's hey nonny no, nonny ninny oh
Then all they miss is Dad

Consider the corn, consider the wine,
One has a day when it's in its prime
The other takes years to be sturdy and fine
If only the two could intertwine
Corn wine, corn wine

An old man sits thinkin'
'Bout the game his life has played
It's hey nonny no, nonny ninny oh,
He needs both nurse and maid

An old woman's takin' care of
One she's loved so long
It's hey nonny no, nonny ninny oh,
And an ending for this song

Consider the corn, consider the wine,
One's in a hurry, the other takes time
One's on a stalk, the other's on a vine
If only the two could just combine
Corn wine, corn wine

LOCO MAN
H. Shearer

Loco man
Watchin' all the fish swim away
He no work, he just sleep and play
Sittin' here on the sand

Sunny land
Coconut comin' down all the time
Milk, she sweeter than honey wine
Sittin' here on the sand

(He's a loco man!)

Loco man
Crazy, but he got a plan
Doin' it just because he can
Yeah, he loco like ice-cold cocoa

Loco man
Sit in sun when he want to sweat
Go in ocean to get him wet
Sittin' here on the sand

(He's a loco man!)

NEVER DID NO WANDERIN'
M. McKean & H. Shearer

My mama was the cold north wind,
My daddy was the son
Of a railroad man from west of hell
Where the trains don't even run

Never heard the whistle of a south-bound freight
Or the singing of its drivin' wheel

No I never did no wanderin'
Never did no wanderin'
Never did no wanderin'
After all

They say the highway's just one big road
And it goes from here to there
And they say you carry a heavy load
When you're rollin' down the line somewhere

Never seen the dance of the telephone poles
As they go whizzin' by

No I never did no wanderin'
Never did no wanderin'
Never did no wanderin'
After all

Never did no wanderin' high
Never did no wanderin' low

Now a sailor's life is a life for him
But it never was for me
And I've never soared where the hawk may soar
Or seen what the hawk may see

Never hiked to heaven on a mountain trail
Never rode on a river's rage

No, I never did no wanderin'
Never did no wanderin'
Never did no wanderin'
After all

OLD JOE'S PLACE
C. Guest, M. McKean & H. Shearer

Whenever I'm out wanderin'
Chasin' a rainbow dream
I often stop and think about
A place I've never seen
Where friendly folks can gather
And raise the rafters high
With songs and tales of yesteryear
Until they say goodbye

Well there's a puppy in the parlor
And a skillet on the stove
And a smelly old blanket
That a Navajo wove
There's chicken on the table
But you gotta say grace
There's always something cookin'
At Old Joe's Place

Now folks come by 'round evenin' time
Soon as the sun goes down
Some drop in from right next door
And some from out of town

(Pick it!)

Well there's a puppy in the parlor
And a skillet on the stove
And a smelly old blanket
That a Navajo wove
There's popcorn in the popper
And a porker in the pot
There's pie in the pantry
And the coffee's always hot
There's chicken on the table
But you gotta say grace
There's always something cookin'
At Old Joe's Place

Now they don't allow no frowns inside
Leave them by the door
There's apple brandy by the keg
And sawdust on the floor
So if you've got a hankerin'
I'll tell you where to go
Just look for the busted neon sign
That flashes "Ea—a—oe's"

Well there's a puppy in the parlor
And a skillet on the stove
And a smelly old blanket
That a Navajo wove
There's popcorn in the popper
And a porker in the pot
There's pie in the pantry
And the coffee's always hot
There's sausage in the morning
And a party every night
There's a nurse on duty
If you don't feel right
There's chicken on the table
But you gotta say grace
There's always something cookin'
At Old Joe's Place

SKELETONS OF QUINTO
C. Guest

I worked the fields my father worked
From dawn 'til setting sun
My calloused hands and wind-burned face
Have marked me as a man
Who has no voice, no rights, no hope
No place to call his own
And the skeletons of Quinto call me home

(English)
The silver tentacles of the moon's rays
Haunt me
The deathly silence of the mountains
Chills me to the bone
And the skeletons of Quinto call me home

(Spanish)
Los tentaculos plateados de los
Rayos de la luna me persiguen
El silencio mortál de las montañas
Me estremecen hasta los huesos
Y los esqueletos de Quinto me llaman a morada

If I live to be a hundred
I won't know mi papa's plight
The cruelty of the master's whip
The horrors of the night
He braved them all and stood his ground
The bravest ever known
And the skeletons of Quinto call me home

(English)
An ocean of shame stirs our memories
The strangled nightmares of death
Chill me to the bone
And the skeletons of Quinto call me home

(Spanish)
Un océano de verguenza incita nuestros recuerdos
Las estranguladas pesadillas de muerte
Me estremecen hasta los huesos
Y los esqueletos de Quinto me llaman a mi morada

I know that somehow in this world
The workers must be free
That toil and sweat and tyranny
The fascist jeu d'esprit
Will only serve to keep us down
And aid the bourgeoisie
And the skeletons of Quinto call me home

Note: Autoharp plays song in D minor and is tuned down a minor third

Catheter Song

Words and Music by
CATHERINE O'HARA

Catheter Song *continued*

Killington Hill

Words and Music by
MICHAEL McKEAN

Killington Hill *continued*

Killington Hill *continued*

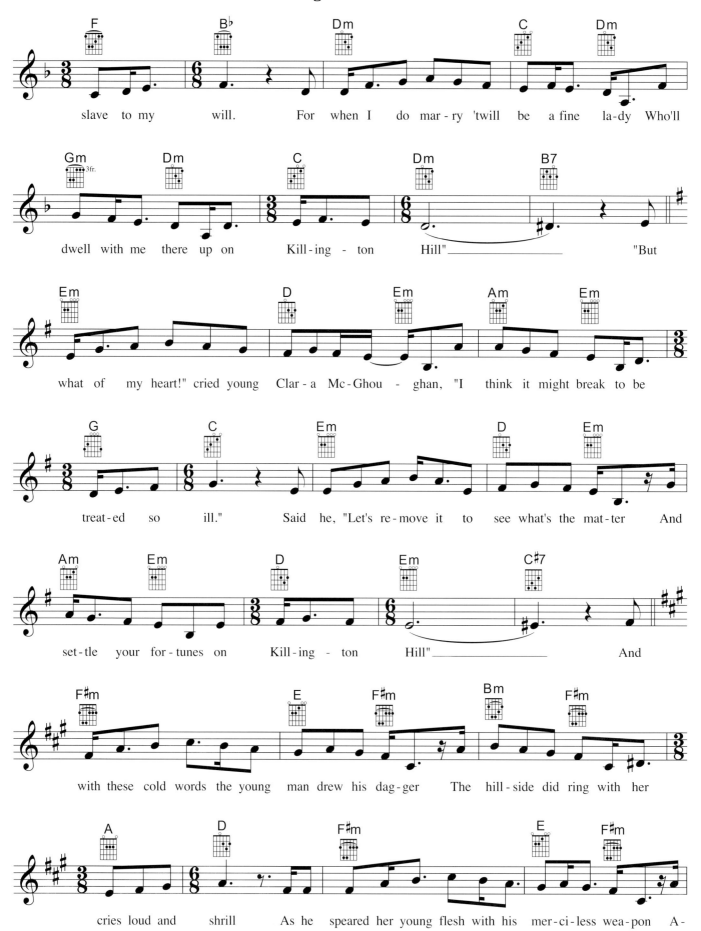

slave to my will. For when I do mar-ry 'twill be a fine la-dy Who'll

dwell with me there up on Kill-ing - ton Hill" _____ "But

what of my heart!" cried young Clar-a Mc-Ghou - ghan, "I think it might break to be

treat-ed so ill." Said he, "Let's re-move it to see what's the mat-ter And

set-tle your for-tunes on Kill-ing - ton Hill" _____ And

with these cold words the young man drew his dag-ger The hill-side did ring with her

cries loud and shrill As he speared her young flesh with his mer-ci-less wea-pon A-

Killington Hill *continued*

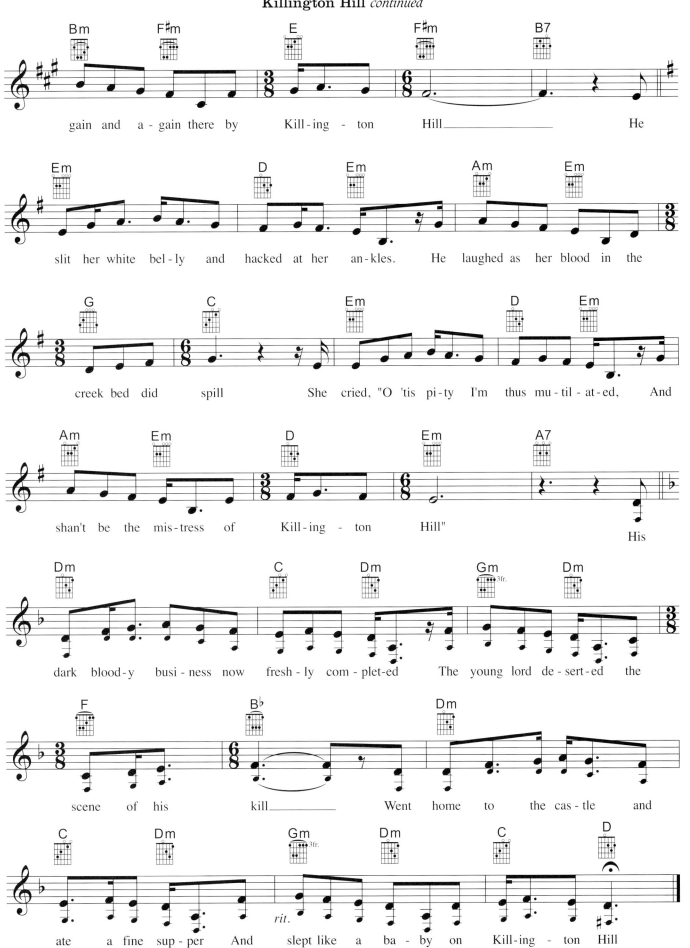

gain and a-gain there by Kill-ing-ton Hill_____ He

slit her white bel-ly and hacked at her an-kles. He laughed as her blood in the

creek bed did spill She cried, "O 'tis pi-ty I'm thus mu-til-at-ed, And

shan't be the mis-tress of Kill-ing-ton Hill" His

dark blood-y busi-ness now fresh-ly com-plet-ed The young lord de-sert-ed the

scene of his kill_____ Went home to the cas-tle and

rit.

ate a fine sup-per And slept like a ba-by on Kill-ing-ton Hill

A Kiss at the End of the Rainbow

Words and Music by
MICHAEL McKEAN
and ANNETTE O'TOOLE

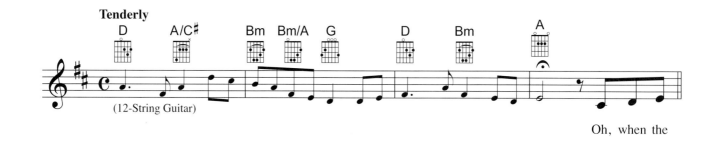

(12-String Guitar)

Oh, when the

veil of dreams has lift-ed   And the fair-y tales have all been told   There's a

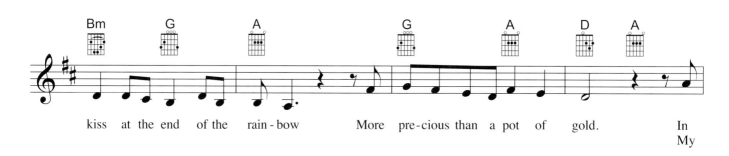

kiss at the end of the rain-bow   More pre-cious than a pot of gold.   In
My

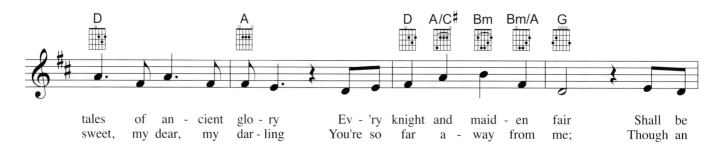

tales of an-cient glo-ry   Ev-'ry knight and maid-en fair   Shall be
sweet, my dear, my dar-ling   You're so far a-way from me;   Though an

joined when the quest is ov-er   And a kiss is the oath that they swear.   And when the
o - cean of tears di-vides us   Let the bridge of our love span the

A Kiss at the End of the Rainbow *continued*

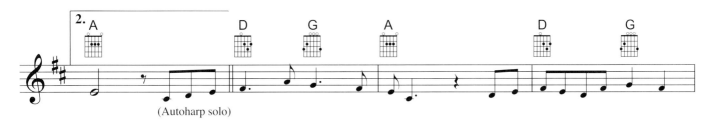

(Autoharp solo)

sea.

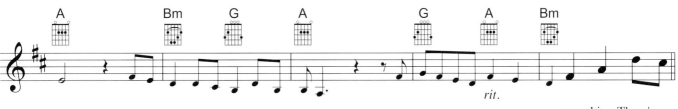

rit.

...your kiss, There's a

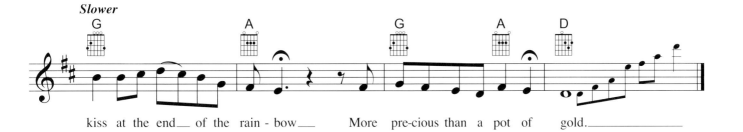

Slower

kiss at the end___ of the rain - bow___ More pre-cious than a pot of gold.___

One More Time

Words and Music by
CATHERINE O'HARA
and EUGENE LEVY

Moderately Slow

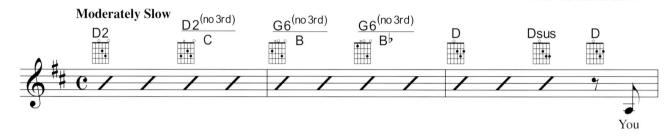

You

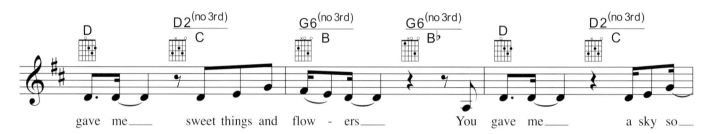

gave me ___ sweet things and flow-ers ___ You gave me ___ a sky so ___

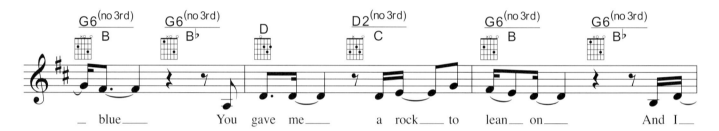

___ blue ___ You gave me ___ a rock ___ to lean ___ on ___ And I

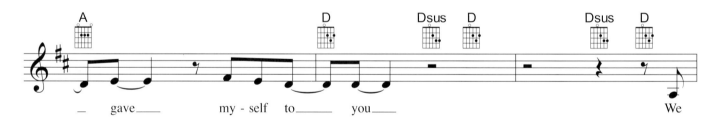

___ gave ___ my-self to ___ you ___ We

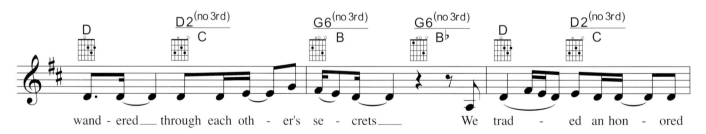

wand-ered ___ through each oth-er's se-crets ___ We trad-ed an hon-ored

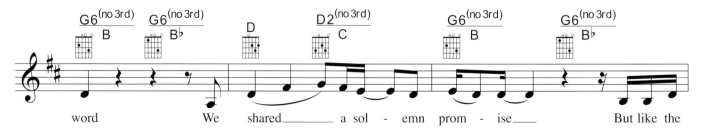

word   We shared ___ a sol-emn prom-ise ___ But like the

One More Time *continued*

One More Time *continued*

One More Time *continued*

life - time____ And what you give____ you just can't take____ a - way____

_____ And I can't take a - way____ my love____ dear____

One mis - take____ is not a crime____ Let's start a - gain____ my love is

yours dear Your love is mine, one more time.____

rit.

The Ballad of Bobby and June

Words and Music by
EUGENE LEVY

The Ballad of Bobby and June *continued*

The Ballad of Bobby and June *continued*

The Ballad of Bobby and June *continued*

Of some-one ap - proach-ing their boots scrap-ing on the ground   As she looked out the

win-dow her heart pound-ed in   her breast   A bro - ken young

Bob - by was clutch-ing a   wounded _____ chest _____   She ran out to

help ease his pain____   He looked up and whis-pered her name   Then she cra-dled his

head in her arms and he smiled____ When he heard his June say   Stay____ with me

Bob-by Don't go a - way____ from me now____ I want you to say____ that you love_

__ me Don't go a - way____ from me now____ I want you to stay____

I want you to stay_____

When You're Next to Me

Words and Music by
EUGENE LEVY

When You're Next to Me *continued*

This love for you____ I'm feel-ing has a pow-er that____ is heal-ing, It can

mend the dark - est hour____ with glorious_____ light When I

taste____ your lips so____ sweet I see beg-gars dine and the sands____ of time up and

stop When I taste____ your lips so____ sweet Black and white band, Ev-'ry dove____

____ lands at your feet____ When you're next to me____ (Autoharp solo)

This love for you____ I'm feel-ing has a pow-er that____ is heal-ing, It can

When You're Next to Me *continued*

mend the dark - est hour___ with glorious_____ light

When I'm ly - ing next to you   I feel moon - beams burn, I see

rain - bows turn in - to gold___ When I'm ly - ing next to you   I hear

an - gels play, I see sweet - er___ days, I see riv - ers___ wind, Through the

end   of time, I see hat - red fall   from the high - est hill, I see

God's good grace shin - ing in_____ your eyes   That's what I see___

___   When you're next to me___

SONG LYRICS

CATHETER SONG
C. O'Hara

Piston or bulb syringe
Won't make your patients cringe

Sure Flo Sure Flo

Don't leave them sore and damp
Use our buttocks drape and penis clamp

Sure Flo Sure Flo
Less time with patients means you're on the go

Single or staggered eyes
Won't cause their hateful cries

Sure Flo Sure Flo

Bags for bedside leg or hip
Color-coded whistle tip

Show them with Sure Flo that you're in the know

Sure Flo Sure Flo

KILLINGTON HILL
M. McKean

In a deep lonely brook near the town of
    Dunfallen
Where the wandering currents do never lie still
Lay the white naked bones of sweet Clara
    McGhoughan
In the dark moisty shadow of Killington Hill

The second-born daughter of farmer
    McGhoughan
As fresh as the dew in the new morning's chill
In love with the son of the aged Lord Bantry
Who held ancient title to Killington Hill

The lovers they'd meet by the cool running water
And drink from each other their love-thirst to
    kill
Then watch the moon rise like a Nesselrode
    biscuit
O'er the whispering treetops of Killington Hill

Said she one cool ev'ning, "Love, when shall we
    marry
For though I am patient I dream of it still
I long to be known as the good Lady Bantry
And dwell in the great hall at Killington Hill"

Said he, "Don't be silly my dear foolish poppet,
You're naught but a plaything and slave to my
    will.
For when I do marry 'twill be a fine lady
Who'll dwell with me there upon Killington Hill"

"But what of my heart!" cried young Clara
    McGhoughan,
"I think it might break to be treated so ill."
Said he, "Let's remove it to see what's the
    matter
And settle your fortunes on Killington Hill"

And with these cold words the young man drew
    his dagger
The hillside did ring with her cries loud and
    shrill
As he speared her young flesh with his merci-
    less weapon
Again and again there by Killington Hill

He slit her white belly and hacked at her ankles
He laughed as her blood in the creek bed did
    spill
She cried, "O 'tis pity I'm thus mutilated
And shan't be the mistress of Killington Hill"

His dark bloody business now freshly completed
The young lord deserted the scene of his kill
Went home to the castle and ate a fine supper
And slept like a baby on Killington Hill

A KISS AT THE END OF THE RAINBOW
M. McKean & A. O'Toole

Oh, when the veil of dreams has lifted
And the fairy tales have all been told
There's a kiss at the end of the rainbow
More precious than a pot of gold

In tales of ancient glory
Every knight and maiden fair
Shall be joined when the quest is over
And a kiss is the oath that they swear

And when the veil of dreams has lifted
And the fairy tales have all been told,
There's a kiss at the end of the rainbow
More precious than a pot of gold.

My sweet, my dear, my darling
You're so far away from me;
Though an ocean of tears divides us
Let the bridge of our love span the sea.

And when the veil of dreams has lifted
And the fairy tales have all been told
There's a kiss at the end of the rainbow
More precious than a pot of gold.

ONE MORE TIME
C. O'Hara & E. Levy

You gave me sweet things and flowers
You gave me a sky so blue
You gave me a rock to lean on
And I gave myself to you

We wandered through each other's secrets
We traded an honored word
We shared a solemn promise
But like the raven's cry it must be heard.

Please don't take away your love dear
One mistake is not a crime
Let's start again my love is yours dear
Your love is mine, one more time

You tell me a cold wind's a-comin'
A chill that turns a heart to stone
And your eyes say it's time to move on
Down a road you'd rather walk alone.

Now pride is a raging river
It can fell the tallest tree
But a song 'neath the wings of forgiveness
Can tame the stormy sea

Please don't take away your love dear
One mistake is not a crime
Let's start again my love is yours dear
Your love is mine, one more time

They say that nothing lasts forever
Like the tide that comes in but doesn't stay
But our journey has taken up a lifetime
And what you give you just can't take away

And I can't take away my love dear
One mistake is not a crime
Let's start again my love is yours dear
Your love is mine, one more time

THE BALLAD OF BOBBY AND JUNE
E. Levy

This is the story of Bobby and June
A boy and a girl who kidnapped the moon
But they fell in love to the sound
Of guns
The year was 1861

The army came looking for men to recruit
Dressing boys up like soldiers in blue Union
    suits
Take this sword and cut down Johnny Reb
They said
You'll come back a hero or you'll come back
    dead

Stay with me Bobby
Don't go away from me now
I want you to say that you love me
Don't go away from me now
I want you to stay

Now Bobby he marched to the eye of a storm
The blue coats were falling the blood was still
    warm
A battle was raging and the only thing in
His eyes
Was the thought of his June and making it
    home alive

His army outnumbered they started to run
When Bobby went down with the crack of a gun
And as he lay still his face sinking in
The rain
He knew that he never and ever would see June
    again.

Stay with me Bobby
Don't go away from me now
I want you to say that you love me
Don't go away from me now
I want you to stay

It was the morning of Christmas when June
    heard a sound
Of someone approaching their boots scraping
    on the ground
As she looked out the window her heart
    pounded in
Her breast
A broken young Bobby was clutching
A wounded chest

She ran out to help ease his pain
He looked up and whispered her name
Then she cradled his head in her arms
And he smiled
When he heard his June say

Stay with me Bobby
Don't go away from me now
I want you to say that you love me
Don't go away from me now
I want you to stay

WHEN YOU'RE NEXT TO ME
E. Levy

When I'm standing next to you
There's a song to sing
I know everything's
Feeling right
When I'm standing next to you
Steeple bells ring
Only good things
Do I see
When you're next to me

When I hold your hand in mine
A different world wakes
A new morning breaks
With the sun
When I hold your hand in mine
Children's dreams take flight
Through a star-lit night
That's what I see
When you're next to me

This love for you I'm feeling
Has a power that is healing
It can men the darkest hour
With glorious light

When I taste your lips so sweet
I see beggars dine
And the sands of time
Up and stop
When I taste your lips so sweet
Black and white band
Every dove lands
At your feet
When you're next to me

This love for you I'm feeling
Has a power that is healing
It can men the darkest hour
With glorious light

When I'm lying next to you
I feel moonbeams burn
I see rainbows turn
Into gold
When I'm lying next to you
I hear angels play
I see sweeter days
I see rivers wind
Through the end of time
I see hatred fall
From the highest hill
I see God's good grace
Shining in your eyes
That's what I see
When you're next to me

Fare Away

**Words and Music by
CJ VANSTON, MICHAEL McKEAN
and ANNETTE O'TOOLE**

Sun breaks o-ver the sprits'-l yard,_____
Cap-tain's stalk-ing the quar-ter-deck_____

Jib sheets haul-in' to lee-ward hard._____
Tells the tale of his first ship-wreck._____

Cross-trees hum-min' a morn-in' hymn._____
Cast a-way with a case of rum;_____

I'm the cab-in boy, call me Jim.
Hoped that res-cue would nev-er come.

Fare a-way, fare a-way, Un-der main top-sail, To the fur-be-low of the wi-ly

1. whale._____

2. whale. To the

Fare Away *continued*

fur - be - low of the wi - ly, wi - ly...

(Penny Whistle)

rit.

Faster (Ship's Bell) *a tempo*

(Accordion)

First mate Ad-am's a hard-ened man_____ Says the cap-tain's a char - la - tan_____

_____ Don't know tac-kle from fut - tock plates_____ He'll

sail us in-to the Pearly_____ Gates. Fare a -

way, fare a - way, Un - der main top - sail, To the fur - be - low of the wi - ly

Fare Away *continued*

Just That Kinda Day

**Words and Music by
CHRISTOPHER GUEST and
MICHAEL McKEAN**

Just That Kinda Day *continued*

Don't cry, don't fret, don't frown,___ you'll on - ly bruise___ your heart.___

The sun's a cir - cus clown,___ the moon's a lem - on tart.___

(Whistle)

D.S. al Coda

(Guitar)

Let's give our - selves a break___ from sor - row and___ dis - may.___

The world's a birth-day cake,___ it's just that kind - a day!___ It's

just that kind - a day!___ It's just that kind - a

day!___ Hmm

Main Street Rag

Words and Music by
JOHN MICHAEL HIGGINS

A - walk-in' down to Main Street ev - 'ry - bo - dy's gon - na sing____

The moth-ers and the broth-ers ev - 'ry - bo - dy let-tin' free-dom ring____

____ I'll put your hand in mine____ Gon-na have us all

one fine time We're the Main Street Sing - ers and we're here to make a cra-zy scene____

How far out can Main Street get?____

...can____ Main____ Street get? whoa yeah!!!!

Potato's in the Paddy Wagon

Words and Music by
MICHAEL McKEAN
and ANNETTE O'TOOLE

Potato's in the Paddy Wagon *continued*

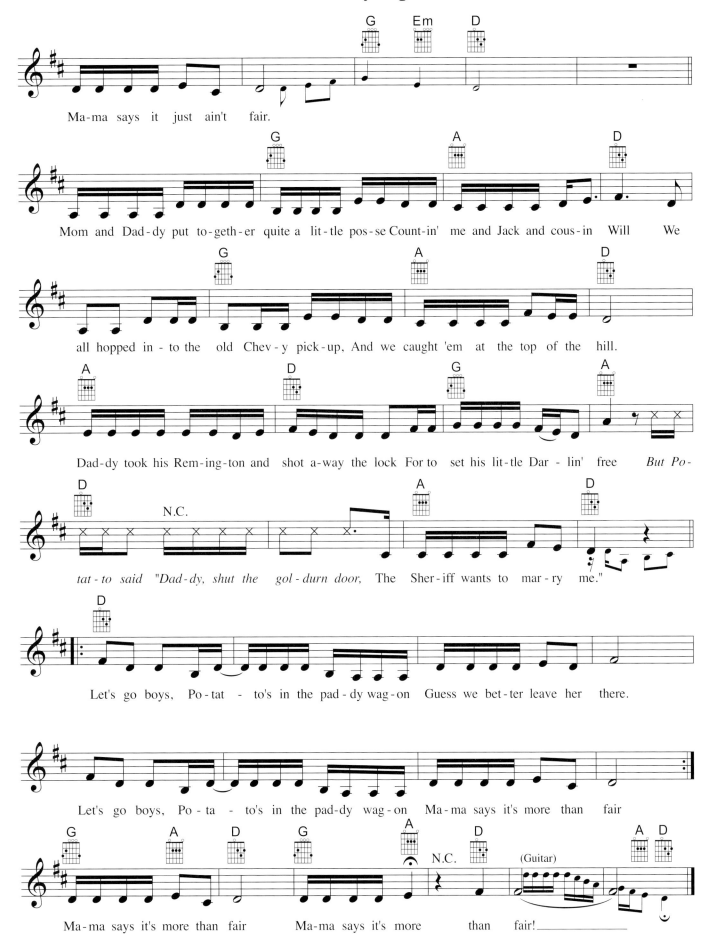

The Good Book Song

Words and Music by
MICHAEL McKEAN
and HARRY SHEARER

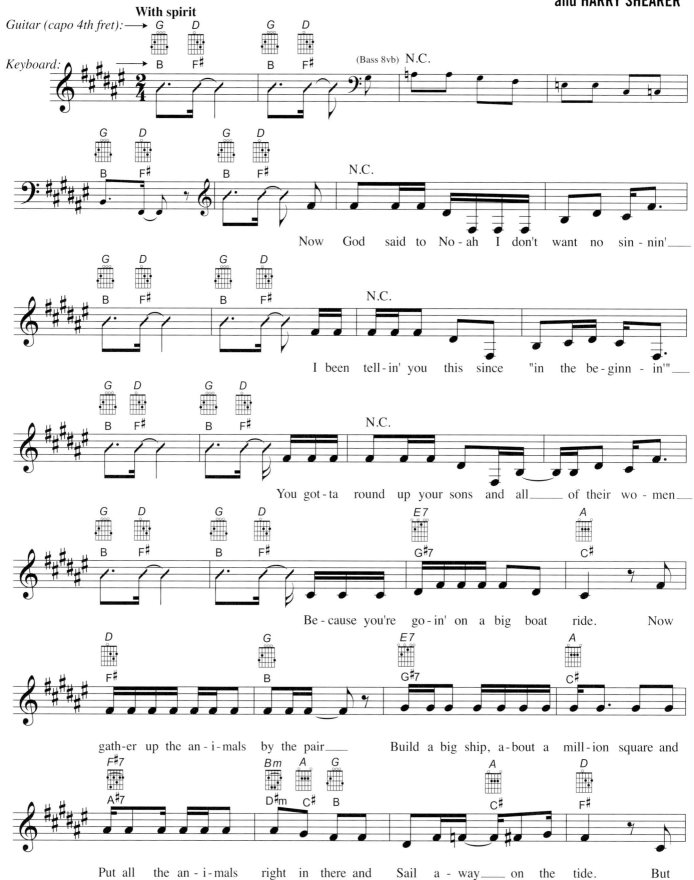

The Good Book Song *continued*

The Good Book Song *continued*

Optional Verse 2

Said Old Man Moses to the Hebrew chillun
"I know the road is long and the pace is killin'
But if the spirit's strong and the flesh is willin'
We can surely make the final push!

"And after forty years of heat and sand
We can rest our bones in the Promised Land
A glorious future has all been planned:
I heard it from a burning bush."

But what if Moses
Had stuck to roses?

We'd wander still from hill to hill
No cooling shade, no lemonade,
No Independence Day parade! (Awwww. . .)
It's scary but it's true

(Chorus)

THE NEW MAIN STREET SINGERS

SONG LYRICS

FARE AWAY

CJ Vanston, M. McKean & Annette O'Toole

Sun breaks over the sprits'l yard,
Jib sheets haulin' to leeward hard.
Crosstrees hummin' a mornin' hymn.
I'm the cabin boy, call me Jim.

Fare away, fare away,
Under main topsail
To the furbelow of the wily whale.

Captain's stalking the quarterdeck
Tells the tale of his first shipwreck.
Cast away with a case of rum;
Hoped that rescue would never come.

Fare away, fare away,
Under main topsail,
To the furbelow of the wily whale,
To the furbelow of the wily, wily...

First mate Adam's a hardened man
Says the captain's a charlatan
Don't know tackle from futtock plates
He'll sail us into the Pearly Gates.

Fare away, fare away,
Under main topsail
To the furbelow of the wily whale.

I been sailin' these seven seas
Since I's nigh-high to a mermaid's knees
Come next April I'm sixty-three
I can't advance, I like short pants
Safe in the cabin on the open sea.
Safe in the cabin on the open sea.

Fare away, fare away,
Under main topsail,
To the furbelow of the wily whale.
To the furbelow of the wily whale.
To the furbelow of the wily, wily whale.

JUST THAT KINDA DAY

C. Guest & M. McKean

It's just that kinda day.
It's time to kick on back, toss your cares away.
Cartwheels and piggybacks, it's just that kinda
    day.

Tell mean old Mister Blues he's welcome here no
    more.
Put on your happy shoes and chase him out the
    door.

Today when I awoke
All my cares went up in smoke
I thought about the sad-eyed folk
Who've never heard this song

Don't cry, don't fret, don't frown, you'll only
    bruise your heart.
The sun's a circus clown, the moon's a lemon
    tart.

I'm sittin' on a hill, a-watchin' clouds at play.
Love clouds, I always will; it's just that kinda
    day.

Let's give ourselves a break from sorrow and
    dismay.
The world's a birthday cake, it's just that kinda
    day!

It's just that kinda day!
It's just that kinda day!

MAIN STREET RAG

J. M. Higgins

A-walkin' down to Main Street
Everybody's gonna sing
The mothers and the brothers
Everybody lettin' freedom ring

I'll put your hand in mine
Gonna have us all one fine time

We're the Main Street Singers
And we're here to make a crazy scene
How far out
Can Main Street get?
Whoa yeah!

POTATO'S IN THE PADDY WAGON
M. McKean & A. O'Toole

Come on boys, Potato's in the paddy wagon
Gotta get her outta there.
Come on boys, Potato's in the paddy wagon
Mama says it just ain't fair.

One night Mama went to fetch us up a sweet
    potato
Fell down the cellar stairs.
Stork dropped in while she was on the floor
So my sister was born down there.
Daddy said this'n'll be nothin' but a mis'ry
Never will be worth a damn.
But Mama just loved her little sweet
    potato baby
With a face like a parboiled yam.

Come on boys, Potato's in the paddy wagon
Gotta get her outta there.
Come on boys, Potato's in the paddy wagon
Mama says it just ain't fair.

Potato grew up to be as pretty as a peach
In her calico and honey-yella curls
Went to the Apple Cider Ball at the arm'ry
With all the other ripe and ready girls
Sheriff Dan Pike picked Potato for the polka
But she spurned him with a fiddle-dee-dee
And before she could turn around and find
    another partner
Sheriff took her into cust-o-dee.

Come on boys, Potato's in the paddy wagon
Gotta get her outta there.
Come on boys, Potato's in the paddy wagon
Mama says it just ain't fair.

Mom and Daddy put together quite a little
    posse
Countin' me and Jack and cousin Will
We all hopped into the old Chevy pickup,
And we caught 'em at the top of the hill.
Daddy took his Remington and shot away the
    lock
For to set his little Darlin' free
But Potato said, "Daddy, shut the gol-durn door,
The Sheriff wants to marry me."

Let's go boys, Potato's in the paddy wagon
Guess we better leave her there
Let's go boys, Potato's in the paddy wagon
Mama says it's more than fair!

THE GOOD BOOK SONG
M. McKean & H. Shearer

Now God said to Noah, I don't want no sinnin'
I been tellin' you this since "in the beginnin'"
You gotta round up your sons and all of their
    women
Because you're goin' on a big boat ride.

Now gather up the animals by the pair
Build a big ship, about a million square and
Put all the animals right in there and
Sail away on the tide.

But what if Noah
Had just said "no-suh"?

Oh well we'd all have fins and scaly skins
And we'd breathe through gills instead of
    nostrils
And eat fish food 'stead of vitamin pills
It's scary but it's true

So do what the good book,
Do what the good book,
Do what the good book tells you to.

Said Old Man Moses to the Hebrew chillun
"I know the road is long and the pace is killin'
But if the spirit's strong and the flesh is willin'
We can surely make the final push!

"And after forty years of heat and sand
We can rest our bones in the Promised Land
A glorious future has all been planned:
I heard it from a burning bush."

But what if Moses
Had stuck to roses?

We'd wander still from hill to hill
No cooling shade, no lemonade,
No Independence Day parade! (Awwww…)
It's scary but it's true.

So do what the good book,
Do what the good book,
Do what the good book tells you to.

Now God said to David, do you hear that
    drummin'?
You got a great big Philistine army comin'
You wanta oil up your sling and really get it
    hummin'
Because you gotta take the big guy down

Well, David he got a dose of frights,
But he wanted to be king of the Israelites
So he put Goliath right in his sights
And he bounced one off of his crown

But what if David
Had whined and wavered?

We'd live like slaves to Philistine knaves
Our bosses would all be thirty feet tall
And we'd wash their clothes with a fire hose
And sleep in the cracks between their toes
    (Ewwww…)
It's scary but it's true
And if I were you

I'd do what the good book,
Do what the good book,
Do what the good book tells me to!

A Mighty Wind

Words and Music by
EUGENE LEVY, CHRISTOPHER GUEST
and MICHAEL McKEAN

A Mighty Wind *continued*

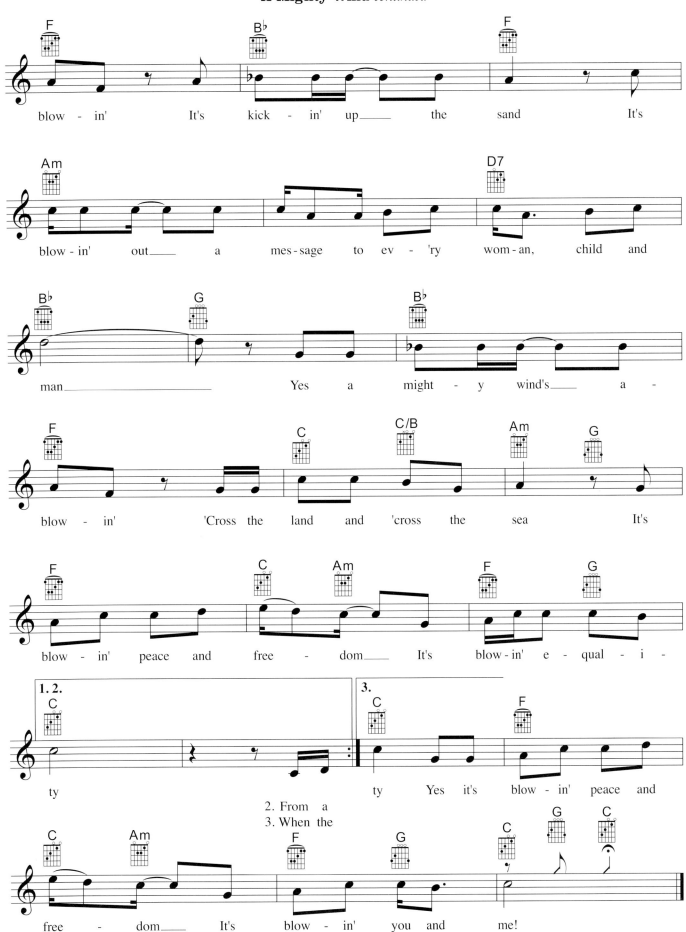

A MIGHTY WIND
E. Levy, C. Guest & M. McKean

As I travel down the back roads
Of this home I love so much
Every carpenter and cowboy
Every lame man on a crutch
They're all talkin' 'bout a feeling
'Bout a taste that's in the air
They're all talkin' 'bout this mighty wind
That's blowin' everywhere

Oh, a mighty wind's a-blowin'
It's kickin' up the sand
It's blowin' out a message
To every woman, child and man
Yes a mighty wind's a-blowin'
'Cross the land and 'cross the sea
It's blowin' peace and freedom
It's blowin' equality

From a lighthouse in Bar Harbor
To a bridge called Golden Gate
From a trawler down in Shreveport
To the shore of one Great Lake
There's a star on the horizon
And it's burnin' like a flare
It's lighting up this mighty wind
That's blowin' everywhere

Oh, a mighty wind's a-blowin'
It's kickin' up the sand
It's blowin' out a message
To every woman, child and man
Yes a mighty wind's a-blowin'
'Cross the land and 'cross the sea
It's blowin' peace and freedom
It's blowin' equality

When the blind man sees the picture
When the deaf man hears the word
When the fisherman stops fishin'
When the hunter spares the herd
We'll still hear the wondrous story
Of a world where people care
The story of this mighty wind
That's blowin' everywhere

Oh, a mighty wind's a-blowin'
It's kickin' up the sand
It's blowin' out a message
To every woman, child and man
Yes, a mighty wind's a-blowin'
'Cross the land and 'cross the sea
It's blowin' peace and freedom
It's blowin' equality
Yes, it's blowin' peace and freedom
It's blowin' you and me!